I0088425

道

大門道

TA·MEN·TAO
THE·TAO·OF·ATHENADORUS

DANAAN PRESS

EY 5.3005 - 5.3039

For the latest information on Danaan Press, its offerings, and on The Danaans and who we are and what we are doing, visit our websites at
www.DanaanPress.com
and *www.TheDanaans.org*

Published by Danaan Press, Inc., in the United States of America.

ISBN: 978-1-890-000-03-5
DANAAN PRESS ID: 001-0310-02120-0

This book, the *Ta Men Tao*, is an expanded restatement, re-interpretation of the *Tao Te Ching* attributed to the quasi-mythical Lao Tzu.

My expansion and restatement is not a literal translation in the scholarly sense: it has been cast in a specifically more poetic way, while bringing forth and fleshing out more fully the Danaan aspects underpinning this great work, in order to present it as the fourth volume in the expanding body of literature which reveals the continuing, continual growth of Goddess-worship among the peoples who treasure the Earth.

道德經, *Tao Te Ching* [*Dào Dé Jīng*]—the "Way of Classic Virtue"—is said to have been written by Lao Tzu ("old boy"), an older contemporary of Confucius, in the 505th Century (6th century BCE). There are no physical remains which can be ascribed to either the body or the life of this Lao Tzu, so it is doubtful that the *Tao Te Ching* was the work of one man, but a compilation of teachings originating in the Taoist school in the kingship of Ch'u.

The *Tao Te Ching* itself barely survived the burning of the books and massacres of the philosophers which the first emperor, Ch'in Shih Huang Ti [Qín Shǐ Huáng Dì], inflicted on the Chinese people. The books of that time were made of thin bamboo strips held together with strings in vertical-columns. Only a few copies of the *Tao* survived the book-burnings, by being buried in the wattle and daub of the mud walls of peasant houses. After the Ch'in Dynasty had been deposed, the books were dug out of the walls. Most of the strings securing the bamboo strips into the correct order, as well as some of the strips themselves, were found to have rotted, and during destruction of the walls to get at the volumes, very many of the remaining strips were separated from the groups to which they belonged. Much effort was put into trying to reassemble the bamboo strips into the correct order, but the *Tao Te Ching* still shows the ravages of the first emperor. I have made no effort to resolve the abrupt changes of topic found in some of the sections (Verse 3 of Poem 36, for example), which were caused by the need to patch the volumes back together: I feel that those are the marks of survival and dedication, and as such are to be cherished.

This text must not be regarded as an attempt at straightforward translation. This should be apparent from its having been given a different name from its primary source. I have had three principle objectives in rewriting the *Tao Te Ching* into the *Ta Men Tao*: to remove the sexist statements which occur in the original, to replace its emphasis on two opposites with the Danaan view of three—of two complements and their interaction— and to fill in some of the poetic holes left by the incomplete restoration done after Ch'in Shi Huang Ti's burning of the books. This restatement of the *Tao Te Ching* in terms of the principles of the Danaan Religion continues forging the bond between the East and West. This process was begun in the *Second Phaedran Letter*, by pairing Danaan Greek and Japanese Shinto terms to show their essential unity, called 大根神道 *Da-Ne-Shin-Tō: the Way of the Deity of the Great Beginning*.

There are some phrases and terms used in the Ta Men Tao which may be unfamiliar to the new reader of my works. Among these are:

The **Passage**, also referred to as **The Path**: 道 *tao* [*dao*] in Chinese, and *tō* in Japanese. The Passage is the mystic path of the fulfillment of the Universe, the mysterious confluence of all statistical possibilities: the realization of the progress of the **Prime Imperative**: the ever-becoming-ness of the Universe.

The Great Gate: the mystic demarcation of the transit of cycle into cycle, progressing through space and time and their interconnectedness.

The Danaan: Greek = Δαναοί, the Danaans /də.néi.əns/, Homeric Greek adjectival form taken from the early, Doric Greek Δᾶ (Classical Γῆ), who is the Classical, Attic Greek Γαῖα, the Goddess as Mother Earth: Δη-μήτηρ, *Demeter*, literally, *Earth-Mother*. Δᾶ (with duplication *Δᾶδα, then consonantal differentiation, *Δᾶρα) is related to other Mother Goddess names: *Tara* of the Celts, *Tara* (*Taraka*) of Hinduism, and *Tara* [*Devi*] of Tantrism.

The Danaans are those who venerate the Goddess and follow the **Prime Imperative** and its Thirteen Freedoms as ethical basis and guide for their actions in living and loving Life and its Earth. **The Prime Imperative** and **the Thirteen Freedoms** are explained in complete quotations extracted from the *First Phædran Letter* for display on the following pages.

I hope this will make the *Ta Men Tao* more enjoyable
and more enlightening.

PER·ILLAM·ÆTERNAM

ATHENADORUS
Ἀθηνάδωρος

A note on pronunciation:

The romanization system used to represent the Chinese pronunciation of the words referenced above is called the *Wade-Giles* system. Despite its illogic and flaws (*e.g.*, *t'* represents an approximate English *t*-sound (or *t* + *h* sound), while *t* stands for *d*, and the letter *d* isn't used), it was the traditional standard for many years in books about the Chinese language that were written in English; therefore, its representation of many Chinese words has become, unfortunately, more or less standard.

The modern *Pinyin* romanization method is far superior, but does require some training in what sounds certain letters represent. In particular, the Westerner must remember that *c*, *j*, *q*, and *x* represent "soft" (*front* or *aspirated*) versions of *ts*, *zh*, *ch*, and *sh* respectively.

Wade-Giles also uses affixed numbers to denote the tone in which the syllable is spoken, whereas Pinyin uses the far simpler method of four diacritical marks that have a close, graphical correlation to the actual intonation of the voice. [The lack of number (or accent) denotes an unaccented, neutral-tone syllable in both systems.]

With that in mind, here are the Wade-Giles and Pinyin versions of the Chinese words and names referenced above:

traditional	duplicated ("simplified")	Wade-Giles:	Pinyin:
大門道	大门道	Ta⁴ Men² Tao⁴	Dà Mén Dào
道德經	道德经	Tao⁴ Te² Ching¹	Dào Dé Jīng
老子	老子	Lao³ Tzu	Lǎo Zi
楚[國]	楚[国]	Ch'u³ [kuo²]	Chǔ [guó]
秦始皇帝	秦始皇帝	Ch'in² Shih³ Huang² Ti⁴	Qín Shǐ Huáng Dì

THE PRIME IMPERATIVE

⊷3 The **Prime Imperative** is that which all nitrogen-based life must obey: that each living entity will live its life in such a way as to maximize the survival chances of Life itself.

There are three constituent Imperatives which, in balance, *are* the Prime Imperative: that one will live its life so as to maximize the survival chances of one's species (*The Natural Imperative*), one's identity group (*The Social Imperative*), and one's self (*The Personal Imperative*).

The **Prime Imperative** is also called the *Contract of Life* or the *Natural Contract*, for, in receiving the gift of Life, proteins and their more advancing forms abide by this requirement called the *Prime Imperative*, established by the Goddess at the very birth of the Universe.

There are Thirteen Freedoms which we Danaans hold to be absolutely essential for humans, for them to be able to follow the **Prime Imperative** fully and freely. These thirteen are the social expression of the operative basis of the **Prime Imperative**.

Definition of the *Prime Imperative*, taken from Athenadorus's *First Phædran Letter*, (in *The Athenadoran Library*) which also explains the phrase *nitrogen-based life*.

THE THIRTEEN FREEDOMS OF THE DANAANS

1 **FREEDOM OF THOUGHT**: that no government shall attempt to control the minds or mental processes of its people.

2 **FREEDOM OF RELIGION**: that no government shall attempt to establish one religion over another.

3 **FREEDOM OF SPEECH**: that no government shall attempt to stifle the free expression and communication of ideas, or the publication of the truth.

4 **FREEDOM OF ASSEMBLY**: that no government shall limit the right and/or ability of the people peacefully to assemble for just and reasonable purpose.

5 **FREEDOM OF PETITION**: that no government shall limit the ability of the people to address themselves to that government for redress of ills and grievances.

6 **FREEDOM OF POLITICAL ASSOCIATION**: that no government shall attempt to infringe on the right of the people to express alternative viewpoints, publicly or through suffrage, or to form associations for the peaceful furtherance of those viewpoints. Nor shall a government restrict suffrage so as to deny any people their right of alternative expression.

7 **FREEDOM OF PERSONAL IDENTITY**: that no government shall take upon itself the right or power to assign or enforce gender roles, careers or attitudes; to legislate prejudicial discrimination; to legislate moralities; to deprive individuals of ultimate control over their own bodies; or to interfere with the private, non-violent activities of consenting adults.

8 **FREEDOM OF PERSONAL SECURITY**: that no government shall disregard the right of the people to be secure in their persons, effects and property, both real and personal , against unwarranted searches, seizures or any other action of that government without public, free and just due process of the law. Nor shall any government abridge the people's right to own and hold private property.

9 **FREEDOM OF PERSONAL INITIATIVE**: that no government shall deny the people, as individuals in equality, the right to strive for the betterment of their lives or conditions of life, in moving forward to the goal of emotional, physical and financial independence, which is the basis of all hope in human life, and of all progress in human society.

10 **FREEDOM FROM HUNGER**: that a society must be responsible for the prevention of hunger among its people.

11 **FREEDOM FROM DESTITUTION**: that a society must be responsible for the prevention of want for basic necessities among its people.

12 **FREEDOM FROM FEAR**: that a society must exercise its powers and abilities to restrain its government from actions and laws that are detrimental to liberty, to inspire that government to enact legislation which will encourage justice and responsibility, and which will discourage violence among its people.

13 **FREEDOM FROM IGNORANCE**: that a society must exert itself fully in striving to educate its people; and must work to diminish the effects and influence of those who espouse ignorance.

Exposition of the *Thirteen Freedoms of the Danaans*, from Athenadorus's *First Phædra Letter*.

1

1 The spirit that has but one name is not the Eternal Spirit.
The name that can be named is not the Eternal Name.

2 The Nameless is the beginning of the Universe.
The All-name is the Mother of the heavens and the Earth.
The Naming is the fulfillment of all destiny.

3 Ever desireless, one feels Her Mystery.
Ever desiring, one sees Her Clarity.
Ever desired, one fulfills the Unity.

4 These three flow from the Origin,
different only in form.

5 The face in darkness:
Shadow-mother of shadow,
Gate of all Mystery.

2

1   All can recognize beauty because they know the Passage.
2   Beauty and non-beauty ebb and flow through the Great Gate:
    the golden portal of distinguishability,
    the sweet grape-cluster of Middle Action—
    where the beautiful and non-beautiful mix and create
    the soul of distinguishing,
    the mind of realization.
3   Who has only slavery knows nothing of freedom:
    Who sees only freedom knows nothing of slavery.
4   It is upon knowledge of both, the co-mingling of waters,
    that stands the Great Hall of the Liberation.
5   Who sees not freedom cannot long to be free.
    Who have not rejected slavery
    cannot cherish the freedom they possess.
6   The Hall of the People is only so strong
    as the will of the people themselves.
7   We know good as good
    because we know the Middle Passage.
8   We have seen the Gate and fathomed its secret:
    it unites the fields as it divides them.
9   Having and not-having are co-equal.
    Difficult and easy are the same.
    Long and short are children of the One.
    High and low are of the same mountain.
    Voice and noise are singers of one song.
    Front and back live in the Unity of the One.
10 Thus We teach and do not teach
    and it is the same.
11 All things rise and fall, never ceasing:
    never ceasing the Passage, joining between.
12 Creating, but not claiming.
    Accomplishing, but never demanding reward.
13 Changes are made,
    and are changed in the making:
    in its tranquility it is eternal.

3

1   Not praising the talented prevents quarreling.
Not amassing treasures prevents stealing.
Ignoring desirable things prevents confusion in the mind.
2   Yet, why should fear of robbery prohibit collecting?
Or fear of confusion prohibit seeking desirable things?
3   The wise will lead by praising the Passage:
for it is in understanding the extremes-inherent
that middle peace is brought to light.
4   We lead therefore by knowing hearts,
channeling ambitions,
strengthening resolve.
5   If the people lack knowledge and the desire for it,
intellectuals cannot interfere:
the people will be moved by fear.
6   Act in non-action
and all will know peace.

4

1   The Passage is a full, flowing spring:
use will never drain it.

2   Boundless Source of the Universe!
Reveal our gentleness!
Simplify our outlook!
Increase our subtlety!
Make us One with your transcendent Universe!

3   Deeply hidden companion,
ever within us,
I know not whence you come:
You are the first Mother of the people!

5

1 The Universe is remorseless:
  the delusions of men are nothingness.
2 The Danaans are remorseless:
  the lies of men are shown to be nothingness.
3 The Earth and the heavens are like a cloud,
  changing in form, but not in self.
4 The more it moves, the more it yields.
5 Learn constancy from the silence:
  stand strong with the Passage.

6

1 The Passage Spirit is immortal:
 She is Woman, Primal Mystery,
 Gateway foundation of the Universe.
2 The Passage is a veil of mist, ephemeral shimmering:
 Path of Cycle into Cycle.
3 Follow Her: She will never fail.

7

1 The Universe lasts forever.
2 How does the Universe last forever?
   Because it knows Birth, yet was not born,
   has felt Death, yet cannot die.
   Thus it is ever alive.
3 We stand at the rear,
   thus we take the lead.
4 We are at one with the past,
   therefore first into the future.
5 We are detached,
   thus at one with all:
   reaching beyond self,
   through the sharing,
   out toward Unity.
6 In the voyage that leads to Unity,
   discover fulfillment.

8

1   The Passage is like water:
      it gives life to the Universe and does not fuss.

2   It flows through all things,
      remembered, not unforgotten.
      And thus is like the Imperative Prime.

3   In living, cherish the Earth.
      In meditation, dive deep into the mind.
      In friendship, be gentle and mindful of the bond.
      In speaking, worship truth.
      In judgment, justice.
      In leading, humility.
      In commerce, competence.

9

1   Better not to fill than to spill.
    The oversharpened blade blunts first.
    Treasures of gold are soonest filched.
2   Claim the undue and disaster follows.
3   Go to sleep when day is done:
    the Moon will hold the sky till morning.

10

1   Mind, body and soul in your Unity,
    can you embrace the One and remain whole?

2   Listening and recognizing ignorance,
    can you return to your childhood?

3   Scrubbing and rinsing away the ancient hatred,
    can you be without stain?

4   Loving all the people and leading the nation,
    can you do so without arrogance?

5   Opening and closing the windows of the Universe,
    can you explain the Unity of the Goddess?

6   Understanding and being receptive to all things,
    can you act in tranquility?

7   To give birth, guidance and nourishment,
    to hold without struggling to possess,
    to labor without demanding recognition,
    to lead without lessening the people's freedom.
    This is the Prime Imperative: mystical virtue.

11

1   All the spokes share the wheel-hub:
    it is the hole that gives it usefulness.

2   Form clay into a bowl:
    it is the volume-possibility within
    that creates utility.

3   Cut doors and windows in the walls that form a room:
    the walls give it substance,
    the holes, purpose.
    And profit lies in the difference between the two.

12

1   The infinite colors can blind,
the infinite tones can deafen,
the infinite flavors can dull the appetite.

2   Ever-racing and hunting destroy tranquility.
Ever-grasping for precious things leads one from the Path.

3   Thus we eat without gorging,
read but do not tire the mind,
show affection when affection is due.

4   Only from the Middle are all boundaries in view.

13

1   Acknowledge failure without despair;
look on misfortune as opportunity in human life:
for the surmounting of calamity
is the triumph of humanity,
and turning to face our problems—
the very soul of victory.

2   Disease is as much a part of life
as ease is integral to existence.

3   As ease is a challenge to self-discipline,
disease is an opportunity to strengthen devotion.

4   Who loves the people more than
ruling the people
can be trusted with the people.

5   Who loves the Earth more than
dominion over the Earth
can be trusted with the life of the Earth.

14

1   The shape invisible, transcending form.
The quiet inaudible, transcending silence.
The grasp intangible, transcending touch.
These are beyond description,
yet are described in the One.

2   Its summit is not blinding,
its base is not obscure.

3   Interconnected streams intertwined
distinct in undecipherability,
becoming again that which is becoming.

4   The formless form,
the shapeless shape,
the unseeable image.

5   The fathoming of shadows,
pottery-molding of mists.

6   Draw near it, you see no beginning.
Draw away from it, you see no end.

7   Preserve the quiet Stream from the Past:
the ability to be One with the Beginning
is the source of Unity with the Passage.

15

1   The ancient ones, well-versed in the Passage
were subtle observers,
mysteriously cognizant,
profoundly powerful.

2   Because we cannot fully fathom their knowledge,
we can only describe its workings:
halting, like those crossing a frozen stream,
cautious, as if realizing the nearness of danger,
formal, like a courteous guest,
yielding, like snow in the sun,
resolute, like the uncarved block,
open, like a mountain valley,
veiled, like a muddy stream.

3   Who can be enfogged and yet quietly await the clearing?
Who can be tranquil until moving with the defense?

4   Who knows the Passage seeks neither starvation
nor to be stuffed full.

5   It is because they knew the Passage
that the ancient ones could be worn out,
then completely made new.

16

1   We commit ourselves to attain peace:
we grasp firmly the rest within quietude.

2   The numberless creatures arise, soaring together:
we are One with their return.

3   Numberless, each returns
to its separate, common origin,
the Origin which is the Self.

4   Returning to the Origin produces tranquility.

5   The Passage of the Return is constant,
constantly evolving:
knowledge of the Constant is the Mother of Wisdom.

6   Wisdom is self-identity within the Goddess.
Willful ignorance is disastrous folly.

7   Who works from knowledge of the Constant
will be led into equanimity,
from equanimity to compassion,
from compassion to love of Nature,
from love of Nature to the Way of the Prime Imperative.

8   And the Way of the Prime Imperative
leads to Oneness with the Goddess,
which is Peace Eternal:
for the Passage will never fail.

17

1   The best ruler is the least ruling:
the most forgotten, the least intruding.
The next is one known and loved.
The next is one feared.
The next is one revolted against.

2   When new laws are made,
more of the old laws will be broken.

3   The best leader is hesitant to speak,
guarding words carefully in all actions:
thus the people will think the accomplishments
were all their own
and that thought will be true.

18

1 When justice and compassion are everywhere present,
  the Passage may be forgotten.
2 When cleverness and selective ignorance are nurtured,
  the great paranoid hypocrisy flourishes.
3 When some family members squabble,
  others will become caring.
4 When the nation is threatened,
  loyal officials will arise.

19

1. Renounce learning,
   and ignorance will no longer trouble you.
2. Renounce wisdom and sagacity,
   and everyone will seem a hundred times more wise.
3. Renounce compassion and benevolence,
   and everyone will seem to be pious and caring again.
4. Renounce ingenuity and profit,
   and bandits and thieves will have no one to rob.
5. These actions deal with outward form only:
   this is not, in itself, enough.
6. Be unaffected, unadorned,
   quiet in warm simplicity,
   fully living the truth of Nature:
   strong like the uncarved block,
   throwing off selfishness by loving the Path:
   moderating ambition and desire.

20

1   How great is the gap between yes and no?
How wide is the gulf between good and evil?

2   Should we fear the nightmares of others? Never!

3   Others seem happy, sharing common festivals,
going to the park in Spring, climbing the terraces.

4   I alone show no movement, reveal no emotion,
like an infant before it awakens to smiles.

5   Without residence, I drift alone.

6   So many have far more than they need—
I alone seem to have nothing.

7   I seem a fool: simplicity seems confused.

8   Others appear to be incisive and clever—
but I, alone, seem plodding and dull:
calm yet restless like the waves of the Sea,
driven like the ceaseless wind.

10   The masses think they have purpose:
they think that I, alone, am aimless,
deserted, despairing.

11   But I am different from all others:
I know the nourishment of the Mother of the Universe.

21

1 In every way, greatest virtue is
   to follow the Passage and only the Passage.
2 The Path is flitting shadow, untouchable.
   Untouchable shadow, yet cradling an image.
3 Shadowy untouchable, yet filled with substance.
   Dim and dark, yet nurturing the Fundament.
4 The Fundament is very Truth,
   within which lies Faith,
   answering, testable.
5 Throughout all ages She has never been forgotten:
   She is the Guide for leading the people.
6 How do I know this?
   From the Passage.

22

1   Yielding to overcome,
bending to straighten,
hollowing to fill,
being worn to renew,
having little to receive benefit:
having too much perplexes.

2   Thus We embrace the Unity
and are an example to the people.

3   Avoiding empty display,
we are conspicuous to all.

4   Not being self-righteous,
we are illustrious.

5   Not bragging,
we attain recognition.

6   Not boasting,
we do not stumble.

7   Because we are not contentious,
we are unified in compassion.

8   We conquer pride to master ourselves.

9   Thus the ancients said,
"Yield if you would overcome."

10   Know yourself:
and your self will be completely yours.

23

1   To talk but sparingly is natural.

2   The wind cannot gust all week,
nor can a rainstorm thunder all month.

3   What is the source of these things?
The Universe.

4   If even the Universe does not create things eternal,
how then can humanity?

5   Therefore, we become One with the Goddess.

6   Who walks the Passage is One with the Passage:
Who is virtuous is one with Virtue.

7   Who is part of the Universe is the Universe.

8   If you do not trust others,
others will not trust you.

24

1   The one on tiptoe is not steady.
Who runs cannot measure the stride.
The arrogant is not circumspect.
The pompous is not respected.
The boaster has no value:
the braggart will not endure.

2   To those at One with the Passage,
these are impediments, useless baggage.

3   These things are detestable bringers of sorrow.
We do not abide them.

25

1   It was mysteriously shaped,
    born before the Universe.
2   Silent in the void,
    existence singular and unchanging,
    presence eternal and ever-changing,
    it is capable of giving birth to all universes.
3   We know not what it calls itself.
    So we call it the Passage,
    and create the term great.
4   Great, it recedes into the distance.
    Recedent, it seems far away.
    Seeming far away, it is also returning.
5   Thus the Passage is great,
    the Universe is great,
    the Earth is great,
    and the people are great.
6   These are the great ones of the Kosmos
    and the people are among them.
7   Humanity moves with the Earth,
    the Earth moves with the Universe,
    the Universe moves with the Passage,
    for the Passage is All-Truth.

26

1   Heaviness is the source of lightness.
       Tranquility is the master of restlessness.
2   Thus the wayfarer on the road
       does not forget to pack for the journey.
3   Though beauty awaits to draw one's eyes away,
       the wayfarer remains unperturbed.
4   Why should the master of 10,000 wisdoms
       act lightly toward that mastery in the eyes of the masses?
5   If light, the root will be lost.
       Lightness will let the base crumble.
6   Restlessness will destroy self-control.

27

1   The good hiker leaves no trace.
    The good speaker leaves no confusion.
    The good counter needs no tally.
2   The best closer needs use no locks,
    yet once closed, it cannot be opened.
3   The best binder knots no cords,
    yet once bound, it cannot be loosed.
4   Thus we have compassion for all people
    and abandon none.
5   We conserve all living things
    and abandon none.
6   This is called following the Passage.
7   The pious teaches the impious.
    The impious is the raw material of the teacher.
8   To disparage the teacher,
    to despise the material,
    each is the source of confusion.
9   These are the foundation of ignorance.

28

1 Know the strength,
  but cherish the tenderness.
2 Be the heart of the Universe.
3 As the heart of the Universe,
  unflagging Truth will be ever with you,
  you who are like little children once more.
4 Know the bright,
  but keep the role of the shadow.
5 Be the ideal of the people.
6 As the ideal of the people,
  constant and steadfast,
  you reunite with the Infinite.
7 Know honor,
  but understand humility and disgrace.
8 Be the fertile valley of the Universe.
9 As the fertile valley of the Universe,
  constancy and incisiveness suffice
  to return to the uncarved block.
10 When the block is worked,
  it splits into many vessels.
11 We use these and become master of Self,
  of the uncarved, carved block:
  the greatest cut does not sever.

29

1   Who would seize the Universe and make it over
    is a restless fool.
2   The Universe is sacred:
    do nothing that might mar it.
3   Who would alter it
    will be ruined in the trying.
4   Who would grasp it
    will lose it.
5   Some lead, some follow,
    some stay behind.
6   Some breathe gently, some breathe fiercely,
    some breathe without design.
7   Some are strong, some are weak,
    some have never tested themselves.
8   Sometimes one destroys, sometimes one is destroyed,
    sometimes one transcends the extremes.
9   We avoid emphasizing the extremes,
    ostentation and arrogance.

30

1 The wise leader does not rattle sabres
to frighten people:
the use of arms always rebounds.

2 Tares and thistles are the legacy of armies encamped.
Hunger is the harvest sown, tended and reaped by war.

3 The best army is disbanded when marching is through.

4 Do only what must be done,
then let the people rest.

5 Get things done:
but do not be pompous.

6 Get things done:
but do not boast.

7 Get things done:
but do not be self-righteous.

8 Get things done:
but not in foolish haste.

9 Get things done:
but never through terror.

10 The strong hurting the weak, young and old,
is going against the Passage.

11 Those not with the Passage
will be overcome by the Passage.

31

1   Powerful weapons are instruments of terror:
we do not trust in them.

2   We give honor to the olive branch in the left hand
over the rifle in the right.

3   Weapons are the tools of terror:
they are unnatural implements.

4   When compelled to use them, it is only
because we have no other choice.

5   There is no glory in conquerors' triumphs,
for they celebrate slaughter.

6   Who exults in battle-gore is not sane.

7   But our Danaan delight
is Freedom within Peace:
of farming the great land, broad and green,
of arts and commerce that make lives and bellies full,
of bright-eyed children's laughter.

8   When people are killed,
we weep for them in sorrow.

9   When victorious in war,
we mourn for those lost by all.

32

1   The Passage is forever limitless.

2   Though at times perceived as small,
it cannot be confined.

3   If the people were able to grasp its meaning,
the Universe would be seen to obey it and no other.

4   Heaven and Earth would be known as One
and the sweet rain of enlightenment would fall.

5   Justice would walk among the people:
natural compassion and respect prevail,
without interfering decree.

6   Once the uncarved block is cut,
the parts need names.

7   Once names are realized,
one must realize when to rest.

8   Knowing when to rest
is liberation from distress.

9   The Passage is to the Universe
as the Ocean is to the rivers:
end, substance and source.

33

1   To understand others is discernment:
to know oneself is wisdom.

2   To subdue others is force:
to conquer oneself is strength paramount.

3   Who has contentment has wealth.
Who perseveres has tenacity.

4   Who maintains resolve will endure.
Who lives at peace will have a full life.

34

1   The Passage flows broad,
to the left, to the right and ahead.

2   All Life depends on it,
yet it demands nothing in return.

3   It brings all tasks to completion,
yet begs no reward.

4   It nourishes the multitude of creatures,
yet binds no lien.

5   Ever selfless in action,
one could call it minute.

6   Yet in not wanting to be master of the multitude dependent,
it is infinite indeed.

7   It is not self-righteous or grasping,
and in that it is truly great.

35

1 Hold to the Passage and all peoples will come to you:
for in you they will find peace and compassion.

2 Casual travelers may be lured by loud music and food,
but the Passage does not entice the multitude
with temporary aromas and fleeting flavors.

3 The Passage cannot be directly observed in its entirety.
The Passage cannot be quickly heard of in its infinity.
Nor can use exhaust it.

36

1   What shrinks must first be large.
    What weakens must first be strong.
    What is thrown off must first be taken up.
    What is received must first be given.

2   This is subtle understanding:
    the yielding and weak can surpass the hard and strong.

3   Fish can survive only surrounded by water:
    the nation's defense will be strong
    only when never put on display.

37

1   The Passage takes no action,
     yet nothing is left undone.

2   If leaders understood this
     all things would occur without struggle.

3   If the leaders still would use force,
     they will be tamed by the uncarved block.

4   The Passage is freedom from obsession.

5   Without obsession, one attains peace of mind
     and all settles in warm tranquility.

38

1   The truly just are just
    because they nurture justice.
2   The foolish try to be just
    because they wish to appear just.
3   The truly benevolent take no action
    yet nothing is left undone.
4   The foolish take many actions
    yet much is left undone.
5   The truly compassionate take action
    only from the loftiest motive.
6   The foolish take action
    only from selfishness.
7   The patriarchal acts officiously,
    and when disproved, retrenches
    and tries to enforce insanity with violence.
8   When the Passage is forgotten,
    compassion remains.
9   When compassion is forgotten,
    kindness remains.
10 When kindness is forgotten,
    reason remains.
11 When reason is forgotten,
    ritual superstition remains.
12 Ritual superstition is the chaff
    of the harvests of the human mind:
    the seed of ignorance.
13 Foreknowledge is only a flower beside the Path:
    to feature it is folly.
14 We assert the substance more than the surface:
    the pulp of the fruit more than the perfume of the flower.
15 Therefore we cherish truth
    and reject falsehood.

39

1   All things have their beginning
in the most ancient One.
2   The heavens are open and clear
through the One.
3   The Earth is perfect and serene
through the One.
4   The divine ones are steadfast and strong
through the One.
5   This vale is wide and fertile
through the One.
6   The multitude of creatures is vibrant and alive
through the One.
7   The people become leaders of the nations
through the One:
their qualities are all drawn
from the Qualities of the One.
8   Without the One, nothing that exists could exist.
9   That which has superiority must have humility,
as well as that in-between.
10   That which is high must also be low
as well as that in-between.
11   Some describe themselves
alone, despised, rejected:
they emphasize the negative-extreme,
forgetting the width of the Path.
12   Too much of that desired destroys desire.
13   Therefore, do not force the future:
all things in their own good time.

40

1 The Passage goes forward by returning.
  Yielding to Truth is the way the Passage moves.
2 The Universe was born from that which is.
  And that which is was born by that
  which always has been.

41

1 The wise student realizes the Prime Imperative
and travels the Passage diligently.

2 The average student hears about the Prime Imperative
and occasionally thinks about the Passage.

3 The foolish student hears of the Prime Imperative
and laughs aloud.

4 If the ignorant did not laugh at it,
the Passage would not be true.

5 Thus it is written that
the brightest seems dim,
the advancing seems to retreat,
the smoothest seems pitted,
the highest seems base,
the purest seems sullied,
the most abundant seems insufficient,
the most robust seems weary,
the most unaffected seems pompous.

6 The perfect square has no corners.
The greatest work takes longest to complete.
The greatest melody is rarely heard.
The greatest existence has no boundaries.

7 The Passage seems hidden and indescribable.
But only the Passage brings about,
nourishes
and carries to completion.

42

1   The Passage begot the One.
    The One begot the Three.
    The Three begot the Nine.
    The All begot the Infinite.

2   The multitude carries yin and embraces yang
    and exists through the Third: the Unity of the One.

3   All people would hate to be alone, despised, rejected,
    yet this is how some try to grasp the devotion of the world.

4   One gains in detracting,
    and becomes detracted in gaining.

5   As others have said, so say I:
    the violent shall meet death in violence.

6   This is the foundation of Her temple.

43

1   The most yielding can conquer
the most obdurate in the Universe:
the intangible penetrating the seemingly impermeable.

2   This is the blessing of non-contention.

3   The tutor who is mute,
the unstruggling laborer.

44

1   Your reputation or your Self—
    which is more important to you?

2   Your Self or your possessions—
    which is more valuable to you?

3   Gain or loss—
    which is more troublesome?

4   The miser will suffer most loss:
    the pecunious will be much bereft.

5   Learn contentment
    and you will never be dissatisfied.

6   Learn when to rest
    and you will not encounter trouble:
    you will persevere.

45

1   The perfect seems flawed,
          but it does not wear with use.
2   The filled seems empty,
          yet it does not drain with drinking.
3   The linear seems curved.
          The wise seems foolish.
          The eloquent seems to stutter.
4   Movement conquers coolness:
          calmness conquers warmth.
5   Calm and clear of vision,
          one can lead the people.

46

1   When the Path is cherished,
    draft-horses work in the fields.

2   When the Path is ignored,
    war-horses trample the crops.

3   There is nothing more destructive than unbridled desire.
    Nothing more calamitous than being discontent.
    No greater affliction than jealous greed.

4   Who knows when to rest
    will always find tranquility.

47

1 Without opening your eyes,
   you can possess the Universe.
2 Without looking out the window,
   you can hold the Path of the Universe.
3 The farther one goes into it,
   the less one knows.
4 Thus we share
   without having to be present,
   understand without struggle,
   achieve without contention.

48

1   In the pursuit of knowledge,
    learn one thing more every day.

2   In following the Passage,
    let go of one thing more every day.

3   One does less and less until nothingness is achieved:
    when nothing at all is done,
    nothing will be left undone.

4   The people are led by not interfering:
    they will not be led by meddling.

49

1   The Danaan is not one mind, alone:
but reaches out, to share the hopes of the people.

2   I see as good those whose actions are good.
I also see as good those whose actions are not good.
Thus we all increase in benevolence.

3   I trust in those who are faithful.
I also trust in those who are not faithful.
Thus we all increase in fidelity.

4   Our message seems intricate,
complicated, confusing.

5   Its simplicity is not apparent to the people
because, like children, they are drawn away
by flashing lights and the pressure of the crowd.

50

1 In choosing between enjoying life and glorifying death,
one of the three now clings to life,
one of the three now charges toward death,
and one of the three travels the Passage—
from transition, through life, to transition.

2 Why is this so?

3 Because the third one has transcended
the base level of short-sightedness.

4 We who know the Passage walk about unafraid:
unafraid of the rhinoceros or tiger,
unafraid of battle wounds.

5 For we cannot be gored without our knowledge,
we cannot be scratched without our approval:
no weapons will pierce us unless we allow it.

6 Why is this so?

7 Because we are One with the Passage.

51

1   In the Passage is all Life.
2   Raised up by energy,
    given form by matter,
    shaped by transformation.
3   Thus all creatures abide in the Prime Imperative
    and honor the Passage:
    not because it has been forced on them
    by laws or words,
    but because the Passage is within the creatures
    and the creatures are One with the Passage.
4   The Prime Imperative creates all living things:
    gives them form and individuality,
    nurses them, guides them, fosters them,
    changes them, develops them, nourishes them.
5   Creating without claiming possession.
    Doing without demanding recompense.
    Leading without interfering.
6   These live in the Primal Mystery.

52

1   The birth of the Universe is the Mother of all that exists.

2   When you understand the Mother,
you will understand Her Children.

3   When you know the Children and are One with the Mother,
you will find liberation from the fear of death.

4   Build a quiet intelligence,
be protective of your senses,
and your life will not be meaningless.

5   Overwhelm your senses,
grow in non-understanding,
and you will have an empty life.

6   Who sees the small is perceptive.
Who yields to conquer is strong.

7   Surrounded by light,
we see the inner glow.

8   Warm within the Passage,
we follow the constant One.

53

1   If I had only the least bit of common sense,
I would still walk only along the great, wide Passage,
and my only concern would be not to stray from it.

2   The great Passage is easily kept to,
yet people call the broad boulevard of ignorance
straight and narrow.

3   Where the government is aloof,
weeds rule the fields
and the granaries stand empty.

4   Still there are those who are showily dressed,
wearing gaudy appointments,
gorged on food and drink:
hoarding possessions.

5   They are the robber-chieftains of the people.

6   This is far from the Path of the Prime Imperative.

54

1   That deeply rooted cannot be pulled up.
    That tightly held cannot slip away.

2   Therefore the honor bestowed
    will be cherished through all generations.

3   Cultivate the Passage in your life,
    and it will be wonderfully alive.

4   Cultivate the Passage in your family,
    and it will be strengthened.

5   Cultivate the Passage in your community,
    and it will prosper.

6   Cultivate the Passage in your nation,
    and it will be honored.

7   Cultivate the Passage in your everything,
    and everything will be recognized in the Unity.

8   Therefore recognize the individual in the individual.
    Recognize the family in the family.
    Recognize the nation in the nation.
    Recognize the everything in the Everything.

9   How do I know the Universe is this way?
    Through the Prime Imperative
    and the fulfillment of the Passage.

55

1   One living the Passage is like the newborn babe:
stinging things are kept far away from it–
wild animals are not permitted to pounce upon it–
soaring birds are not allowed to prey on it.

2   Its bones are weak,
its muscles are weak,
but its grip is strong.

3   It has not enjoyed sexual union,
yet it knows excitement:
its individuality has been established.

4   It can cry all day without becoming hoarse:
because it is in harmony with its existence.

5   To know harmony is to achieve the Constant.
To know constancy is to achieve the Unity.

6   To overemphasize the self is foolishness.
The foolish mind self-centered is the root of violence.

7   The strong hurting the weak, young and old,
is going against the Passage.

8   Those not with the Passage
will be overcome by the Passage.

56

1 Who knows rations words.
  Who blithers has no thoughts.
2 Sit quietly,
  restraining sensations.
3 Find your gentleness,
  simplify your outlook,
  become more subtle.
4 Be One with the transcendent Universe.
  This is the Mystery of the Prime Imperative.
5 Unapproachable and unescapable.
  Unimprovable and undamageable.
  Un-ennoblable and uncursable.
6 Its Unity is the Summit.

57

1   Govern the people with justice.
     Wage war with stealth.
2   The people will be won by protecting their rights.
3   How do I know this? From this:
4   The more laws there are,
     the poorer the people become.
5   The more deadly the weapons are,
     the more fear stalks the land.
6   The more deceitful the people must be,
     the more new lies abound.
7   The more rules and regulations are imposed,
     the more criminals there are.
8   Thus the wise One says,
9   I take no action
     and the people return to the Passage.
10 I am tranquil
     and the people rekindle Justice.
11 I do not interfere
     and the people attain Prosperity.
12 I desire nothing but that the people rediscover Simplicity,
     Forthrightness and Peace.

58

1   When the government acts seldom,
     the people are forthright.

2   When the government acts minutely,
     the people are deceitful.

3   Fortune flowers from misfortune.
     Beneath happiness lies the knowledge of sadness.

4   Who can know how things will be?

5   Truthfulness does not abide forever of itself:
     the truthful can become a liar,
     and fortune become disaster.

6   For many centuries now,
     the children have cherished the disaster of ignorance.

7   We, however,
     perpetuate our fortunate understanding.

8   We are incisive, but do not cut.
     We are piercing, but do not stab.

9   We grow in number, but protect the liberty of all.
     We shine brightly, but do not blind.

59

1   In leading the people of Earth,
there is no gift that surpasses self-control.

2   Using self-control from the beginning,
one follows the Passage.

3   Following the Passage from the beginning,
one lives the Prime Imperative.

4   When one lives the Prime Imperative,
there is nothing that cannot be overcome.

5   Able to overcome all things,
tranquility will ensue.

6   Bestower of tranquility,
one can lead the people.

7   The principles of good government are ever true,
ever the same.

8   Bestowing tranquility to the people
is the great foundation of their affection.

9   The Passage is eternally visible in their affection.

60

1 Leading the people is like handling a cooked fish.
2 Stand before the people within the Passage
    and the impious will lose all power.
3 It is not that they lose their power,
    but that they cannot harm the people.
4 It is not only the impious
    who will not harm the people:
    the wise One as well will not harm the people.
5 The Three will find the benevolence within each other
    and all will be gladdened.

61

1   A great people is like a broad river valley:
collecting the separate streams of existence
into the River of the Unity of Existence.

2   One surpasses another by yielding.

3   Conquering, one may take a lower position.

4   By being pliant, a larger nation can annex the smaller.
The smaller, by yielding, can absorb the larger.

5   Who conquers, yields.

6   The large country would better use its resources.
The small country would provide more for its people.

7   In the balance, each may succeed in its goals.

8   It is a great deed when a larger nation graciously yields.

62

1   The Passage is the Mother of all things.
It is the strength of the pious,
the safe haven of the impious.

2   Flattering words may obtain high rank.
Flattering deeds may purchase promotion.

3   Even so, do not abandon the impious.

4   On the day the Archelaa is raised up
and the councils are installed,
gifts of fine jade and prancing chargers
are not needed.

5   The tranquil gift of the Passage
is the best that can be given.

6   Why has the Passage been loved for so long?
There is no reason other than that
it gives you what you seek,
and does not damn you if you forget.

7   It is the great treasure of the people.

63

1   Act in non-action.
     Accomplish without interfering.
2   Savor that without taste.
     Magnify the small.
     Multiply the few.
     Return benevolence for injury.
3   Do the difficult while still simple:
     build the great up from the small.
4   Complex things arise from the simple.
     The large arises from the small.
5   We strive to understand the simple
     and the small:
     thus become great,
     understanding the complex.
6   Making light promises damages trust.
     Taking all lightly brings on complications.
7   We confront the complicated as complicated,
     still striving to grasp its simple roots:
     and thereby conquer all difficulties.

64

1 Maintain peace while still at peace.
  Deal with trouble before it arises.

2 Still new and brittle is easily broken.
  Still young and small is easily dispersed.

3 Deal with it before it happens:
  keeping in order will prevent disorder.

4 The tree thicker than one's embrace
  arose from tender shoot.

5 The palace nine stories high
  was once a pile of dirt.

6 A journey of a thousand miles
  begins beneath one's own feet.

7 Who contends is defeated.
  Who clutches it will lose it.

8 We are not contentious,
  thus never conquered.

9 We are not clutching,
  thus nothing ever slips away from us.

10 Failure most often rides the verge of success.

11 Nurse the end as well as the beginning,
  then failure will never learn your name.

12 We dare not to be ruled by desire:
  not to care about scarce bric-a-brac,
  not to be afraid of learning new ideas,
  of daring to revive the precious of the past.

13 We dare to help the multitude
  return to Nature
  and cease to contend.

65

1   Some ancients claimed to have knowledge of the Path.
2   They used this claim not to enlighten,
     but to deceive.
3   To lead the people is a great challenge:
     they are not fools.
4   To govern by deception
     is to endanger the nation.
5   To govern without guile
     is to bless the people.
6   These two are the extremes.
7   To recognize the extremes of the Continuum
     is the beginning of mysterious union with the Passage.
8   The Passage is profound,
     ever-extensive, ever-co-extensive.
9   Going, existing and returning with all things,
     creating the great Unity.

66

1   The Ocean receives all waters
    because it is in the lower position.
    Thus it is the master of the rivers.
2   If you would lead the people,
    you must preside with humility.
3   If you would be a good leader,
    be the best follower.
4   With a Danaan leading,
    the people will not know oppression.
5   With a Danaan leading,
    the people's dreams will not find hindrance.
6   Thus the people will give support enthusiastically
    and will not be wearied by it.
7   It is because we are not contentious
    that we are strong in our Unity.

67

1   Some say my teaching
is vast and incomparable.

2   It is vast because of my subject:
there is nothing that can be compared with it.

3   If it were not without equal,
we would long ago have disappeared.

4   There are three treasures I nurture and cherish.
The first is compassion.
The second is thrift.
The third is daring to have humility.

5   Compassion engenders courage.
Thrift bestows generosity.
Humility confers pre-eminence among the people.

6   To abandon compassion for bravado,
to abandon thrift for waste,
to abandon humility for fame,
all will surely lead to death.

7   Compassion gives triumph in battle,
impregnable defense,
and tranquility in all occasions.

8   It is the Goddess nourishing the people.

68

1 The best soldier is not bloodthirsty.
The best fighter is not angry.
The best competitor is not vengeful.
The best employer does not forget humility.
2 This is the strength of non-contention:
the ability to love the people.
3 It is the ultimate sublimity of the Path.

69

1 The strategists often say,
I dare not plan as the host,
but must play the part of the invader.

2 I dare not advance
without knowing retreat as well.

3 This is marching without raising the dust:
rolling up sleeves with no shirt,
defeating the invisible foe,
being armed without bearing arms.

4 There is no disaster greater
than underestimating the resources of the enemy:
doing so has nearly cost us our treasure,
and has cost us many treasured.

5 When two peoples take up arms against each other,
it is the aggrieved one that will prevail.

70

1 My words are clear,
    my precepts easily applied.
2 Yet no one understands them
    or puts them to practice.
3 My words have prehistoric ancestors,
    my actions have a sovereign's discipline.
4 People do not know me:
    they do not dare try to understand.
5 Those who adopt my words are few.
    Those who deride my words are honored.
6 Despite all this, I,
    though wearing homespun and rags,
    conceal the priceless treasure of the Heart.

71

1   To measure one's own ignorance gives strength:
    to disregard one's own ignorance makes weak.
2   Being on guard, one can prevent trouble.
3   We meet no trouble that cannot be tamed.
    For we are ever watchful.

72

1   When the people have lost appreciation
     of the awesomeness of Nature,
     disaster will descend upon them.

2   Do not invade the privacy of the home.
     Do not distress the people's well-being.

3   If you do not overburden them,
     they will not weary.

4   Thus we know ourselves,
     but are not out on display.

5   We have self-respect,
     but are not presumptuous.

6   We have let go of this
     and chosen that.

73

1   The presumptuous brave carries early death.
The humble brave will protect long life.

2   In any moment, death comes to some
and not to others.

3   The course of Nature is the course of Nature.
Why ask That-beyond-Justice for justification?
Even We must sometimes strive with this.

4   The Passage seeks no struggle,
yet always overcomes.

5   It does not speak,
yet answers all questions.

6   It issues no command,
yet is always obeyed.

7   It seems haphazard,
yet is itself Perfect Law.

8   The fabric of the Universe is finitely infinite:
though the weave does not seem tight,
nothing ever slips through.

74

1   If the people do not fear death,
why try to frighten them with the threat of execution?

2   If the people feared death,
and if committing a crime were grounds for execution,
who would dare?

3   There is an official executioner
whose place cannot be usurped.

4   If one would try, it would be like
a novice attempting to cut wood
as if a master carpenter:
few would escape without grief.

75

1   *The people are starving.*

2   *Because the government eats the money in taxes,*
    the people are starving.

3   *The people are rebellious.*

4   *Because the government interferes in their lives,*
    the people are rebellious.

5   *The people are indifferent toward death.*

6   *Because the government uses them as sacrifices,*
    the people are indifferent toward death.

7   *In the cold shadow of the ignorants' boasts,*
    they know better than to cling to life too strongly.

76

1 Humans are pliant, weak when alive,
hard and stiff when dead.

2 Plants are pliable, fragile when alive,
hard and stiff when dead.

3 The hard, unyielding is the disciple of death.
The supple, yielding is the associate of Life.

4 The unadaptive weapon will not help to win.
The straight, unbending tree will know the axe.

5 The stiff, unyielding will be overturned.
The supple, yielding will be victorious.

77

1 The Path is like the testing of a bow:
it lowers the lofty,
it exalts the low,
it decreases the oppressive,
it increases the compassionate,
it exchanges excess and destroys deficit.

2 The Man would do it differently:
he takes from the needy
to give to the wealthy.

3 Who are those who will take their own wealth
and share it with the people?
Only those who know the Passage.

4 Thus we assist without asking recompense,
and do the work without demanding acclaim.

5 This is because our first love
is the liberty within equality.

78

1 There is nothing more yielding and weak on Earth than water.

2 Yet for vanquishing the hard and strong,
nothing can better it,
nothing can approach being its equal.

3 The weak can overcome the strong,
the yielding can overcome the stiff-necked.

4 Everyone knows this fact,
yet no one knows how to use it.

5 Thus I say:
One who takes on the suffering of the people
is fit to be a leader—
worthy of standing before Gaia, the Barley Mother.

6 One who takes on the calamities of the people
is a leader worthy of the name.

7 The truth often at first sounds strange.

79

1   In the dawn of new peace between old enemies,
the haze of mistrust must be removed.
How does one accomplish this?

2   We keep our word,
yet do not demand our due.

3   The compassionate takes over the budget,
the arrogant becomes head-executioner.

4   The Prime Imperative is the Soul of Equality.
The compassionate hold to the Passage forever.

80

1   The smaller the country,
the fewer people it can support.

2   If they arm the militias,
they will not let them use their weapons against each other.

3   If they fear death,
they will not make expeditions.

4   If they possess ships and war-wagons,
they will not make use of them.

5   If they have armor and weapons,
they will hide them.

6   Teach the people to return to innocence:
to enjoy good, ordinary food,
to find comfort in strong, simple clothes,
to be content in warm, quiet homes,
to be tranquil in way of life.

7   Though they live within sight of each other,
and dogs' barking and roosters' crowing
are heard through the trees,
they will live in peace,
and die in peace
without ever having had a fuss.

81

1   The truth does not always seem beautiful.
Beautiful words are often not true.

2   Good words do not always motivate.
Moving words are not always proper.

3   The knowledgeable are often uneducated.
The educated are often in the dark.

4   The wise One is no miser:
having given all, even more is received.

5   Having done much, even more can be done.

6   The Passage is sharp,
yet does not cut:
gives benefit
and does no harm.

7   The Passage bestows all bounty,
and renews all bounty in return.

www.ingramcontent.com/pod-product-compliance
Lightning Source LLC
Chambersburg PA
CBHW060955040426

42445CB00011B/1168